I'm a Christian Now!

Older Kids Activity Book

LifeWay Press®
Nashville, TN 37234

Item 005753858

DEWEY: J248.82
SUBHD: CHILDREN--RELIGIOUS LIFE \ DISCIPLESHIP \ REGENERATION (CHRISTIANITY)

Printed in the United States of America

Kids Ministry Publishing
LifeWay Church Resources
One LifeWay Plaza
Nashville, Tennessee 37234-0172

We believe the Bible has God for its author; salvation for its end; and truth, without any mixture of error, for its matter and that all Scripture is totally true and trustworthy. To review LifeWay's doctrinal guideline, please visit *www.lifeway.com/doctrinalguideline*.

YOU ARE A CHRISTIAN NOW!

What an exciting time in your life! This book will help you understand what it means to be a Christian through fun puzzles and games. Becoming a Christian is a once-in-a-lifetime decision. Being a Christian is a lifetime relationship with God. What Jesus did makes a relationship with God possible. When you become a Christian, you are always a Christian. That relationship makes a difference in how you live your life every day. As you grow, you learn new things all the time. As a Christian, you will be learning new things about God, Jesus, the Bible, your church, and yourself! This book will help you get started.

When you finish this book, you will have a better idea of how to find answers about being a Christian. This book will also help you learn to tell others about Jesus and how He makes a difference in your life.

HOW TO USE THIS BOOK
- Use this book every day.
- Try not to skip a day or do more than one day at a time. Take the time you need to understand the information.
- Find a quiet place.
- Pray, asking God to help you learn what He wants you to know.
- Ask a parent to help you read the words.

THINGS TO HAVE WHEN I USE THIS BOOK
- Bible
- Pen or pencil

THE ABCs
If you need help telling someone about Jesus, remember to review your ABCs.
- A-Admit to God that you are a sinner.
- B-Believe that Jesus is God's only Son.
- C-Confess your faith in Jesus as your Savior and Lord.

CHRISTIAN [KRISS chuhn]
is the name given to a person who has asked Jesus to be his Savior and Lord.

BECOMING A CHRISTIAN

LEARN IT

Read page 48 to find what these words and symbols mean.
Find these four groups of symbols in the grid and circle them.

Crown	Gives		X	God	Cross		We	X		God	Gives	Jesus
Gift	Hands		Sinned	Crown	X		Crown	We		We	Rules	Crown

God	X	Jesus	Crown	Hands	Cross	We	Provided
Respond	Sinned	Gift	God	Gives	Jesus	X	Crown
Jesus	Hands	Cross	We	Rules	Crown	Respond	Gift
Provided	Crown	Gives	Cross	Gift	Hands	Provided	Rules
Sinned	Gift	Hands	Sinned	God	X	God	Cross
Cross	Respond	X	We	Provided	Sinned	Crown	X
Crown	Rules	We	Gift	Cross	God	Gives	Jesus
Gives	Hands	Cross	We	X	Gift	Respond	We
Jesus	God	Provided	Crown	We	Sinned	Rules	Hands

What do each of the symbols mean? Look at page 48 for help.

God rules   Sin   God provides   Jesus gives   we respon

4

BECOMING A CHRISTIAN

Follow the path of each letter to figure out the correct order.
Write the letters in the boxes to reveal the message.

LEARN IT

ABCs OF SALVATION

L E I C N E A O E M T S B I F D V S E

ADMIT: TELL GOD you messed up and you are sorry for doing your own thing and turning away from Him through your thoughts, words, and actions. Repent and turn away from your sin.

BELIEVE: TELL GOD you believe only Jesus can save you and you cannot save yourself from your sin problem.

CONFESS: TELL GOD AND TELL OTHERS that Jesus is your Lord and He is in charge and calling the shots in your life. You are born again into a new life and look forward to being with God forever.

BECOMING A CHRISTIAN

DO IT

Discover the words by adding or subtracting the number of letters. Then match the word to its definition.

A B C D E F G H I J K L M N O P Q R S T U V W X Y Z

E+2, P-1, A+3

☐ ☐ ☐

R+1, F+3, M+1

☐ ☐ ☐

K-1, C+2, R+1, Z-5, R+1

☐ ☐ ☐ ☐ ☐

D-3, A+3, L+1, F+3, V-2

☐ ☐ ☐ ☐ ☐

A+1, C+2, P-4, F+3, C+2, W-1, C+2

☐ ☐ ☐ ☐ ☐ ☐ ☐

E-2, P-1, M+1, H-2, C+2, R+1, R+1

☐ ☐ ☐ ☐ ☐ ☐ ☐

SEPARATES US FROM GOD

TO KNOW AND TRUST THAT SOMETHING IS TRUE

OWN UP TO OR AGREE

TO TELL

CREATOR OF EVERYTHING

GOD'S SON, OUR SAVIOR

BECOMING A CHRISTIAN

Find the symbol along the bottom and the number along the side. Find where each row and column meet and write the corresponding letter in the blank. Find the following verse in your Bible and read it to a family member.

FIND IT

(🌀,4) (ϟ,2) (☀,7) (✚,9) (✳,10) (✿,7) (☘,3) (💧,4) (🧁,8) (💬,1) : (✳,6) (✚,5) (✿,3)

Make a code to share your favorite verse with someone in your family.

10	W	8	I	6	B	J	L	L	L	B
9	L	E	U	H	V	O	V	W	H	I
8	M	F	5	V	O	R	E	Y	J	N
7	O	L	E	A	8	S	X	N	V	I
6	G	T	Y	H	U	K	7	4	V	D
5	M	1	Y	U	N	L	O	Y	C	X
4	N	8	I	4	F	R	D	E	R	M
3	O	P	5	1	D	W	E	G	S	T
2	E	V	G	J	Y	2	V	S	F	L
1	B	J	G	X	T	O	N	M	9	C
	ϟ	✚	💧	✿	🧁	🌀	💬	✳	☀	☘

BECOMING A CHRISTIAN

 LIVE IT Starting with the word "tell," follow the directions, writing each new word in the box beside it. Then move the words with the ✳ into the sentence below.

✳ **TELL**

(CHANGE T TO Y) YELL

(CHANGE SECOND L TO P)

(CHANGE Y TO H)

(CHANGE L TO A)

(CHANGE H TO R)

(CHANGE P TO D)

(CHANGE R TO B)

(CHANGE E TO R)

(CHANGE D TO Y)

(CHANGE B TO P)

As a Christian, I can ___TELL___ others about Jesus, _____

my family, _____ the Bible, and _____ to God.

KNOWING THAT I'M A CHRISTIAN

When you became a Christian, you made the most important decision of your life. Today you will begin to learn what it means to be a Christian!

LEARN IT

WORD BANK:
Admit
Baptism
Believe
Confess
Christian
Holy Spirit
Jesus
Repent
Savior
Sins

DOWN

1. When someone who is already a Christian is lowered into the water and brought back up as a way to show others that he has confessed Jesus as Savior and Lord

2. Name given to people who have confessed Jesus as their Savior and Lord

3. To know and trust that something is true

4. The Spirit of God who helps people understand and receive God's plan of salvation

ACROSS

2. To tell

5. To own up to or to agree

6. God's One and Only Son

7. Actions, attitudes, words, or thoughts that do not please God

8. One who saves others

9. To turn or change from disobeying God to obeying Him

I Thessalonians 5:17 says to pray constantly. Where can you pray?

Fill in names of the places above to find out where you can pray.

A2 _____   D4 _____

B1 _____   C4 _____

D2 _____   C3 _____

C1 _____   A4 _____

The good news is that you can pray anywhere! Pray and thank God for loving you and for sending Jesus. Thank Him for helping you know how to become a Christian.

KNOWING THAT I'M A CHRISTIAN

LEARN IT

Write the answer to each riddle in the box to the left to find the secret word. Write the word in each blank.

☐ First letter of ANIMAL that says MEOW

☐ First letter of the COLOR of a CHERRY

☐ First letter of the MONTH before NOVEMBER

☐ First letter of the bright OBJECT in sky during the DAY

☐ First letter of the SEA ANIMAL that looks like a HORSE

Make a _____ out of a piece of paper. Show the example to a family member and explain how Jesus is our Savior and the person who paid the penalty for our sin.

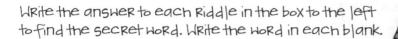

1.
Fold the lower left corner up to the right edge.

2.
Fold the lower right corner up to the left edge to make an upside down house shape.

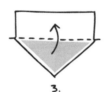

3.
Fold the triangle (house roof) up.

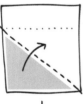

4.
Fold in half at the center point.

5. ←TEAR
Slowly tear straight down the paper at the midway point

6.
Open up the paper to reveal the _____.
Place the _____ in your Bible at Romans 10:9.

KNOWING THAT I'M A CHRISTIAN

FIND IT

Start with the ☼ and move the direction and number of spaces indicated. Each time you discover a letter, write it in the space above the clue. Continue on from that letter to find the message.

Find 1 John 1:9 in your Bible. Say your memory verse to a parent. "If we confess our sins, He is faithful and righteous to forgive us our sins and to cleanse us from all unrighteousness." (1 John 1:9)

Read Acts 11:26 to find out where Jesus' followers were first called Christians. Followers of Jesus were first called Christians in a place called

Thank God for giving Jesus to save you from your sin. Ask Him to help you tell someone about Jesus this week. Write his or her name in the blank.

John 3:16 tells us that

☐ ☐ ☐
↓1←1 ↑3→1 →1↓2

☐ ☐ ☐ ☐ ☐
↑1 ↑1←1 ←2↓2 →3↑2 ↓2

the ☐ ☐ ☐ ☐ ☐
←2 ↑2→1 ↓4 →1↑3 ↓1

KNOWING THAT I'M A CHRISTIAN

KNOWING THAT I'M A CHRISTIAN

Review Your ABCs

LIVE IT

Color the spaces for the **ADMIT** statement in **RED**.
Color the spaces for the **BELIEVE** statement in **BLUE**.
Color the spaces for the **CONFESS** statement in **GREEN**.

ADMIT	THAT	FAITH IN	THAT YOU	ARE	SAVIOR AND	SON.
BELIEVE	TO	JESUS IS	GOD'S	AS YOUR	A	LORD.
CONFESS	YOUR	GOD	JESUS	ONE AND	ONLY	SINNER.

THANK GOD FOR HELPING YOU KNOW HOW TO BECOME A CHRISTIAN.

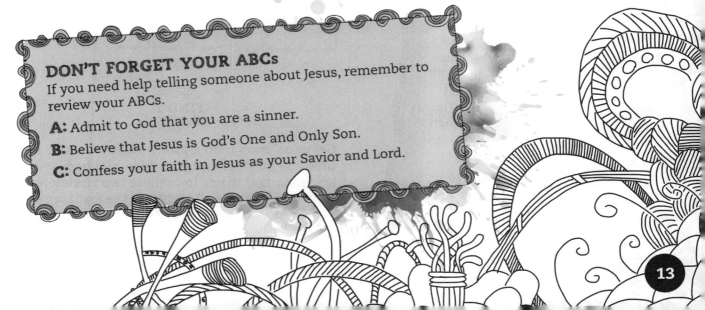

DON'T FORGET YOUR ABCs

If you need help telling someone about Jesus, remember to review your ABCs.

A: Admit to God that you are a sinner.

B: Believe that Jesus is God's One and Only Son.

C: Confess your faith in Jesus as your Savior and Lord.

FOLLOWING JESUS' EXAMPLE

Discover two important things you do after becoming a Christian. Look at the pictures and write the first letter of each word in the blank above the picture. Then unscramble the letters to find out those two things.

LEARN IT

UNSCRAMBLE

UNSCRAMBLE

UNSCRAMBLE

THE LORD'S SUPPER

To help His disciples remember Him, Jesus shared a special meal with them. At the meal He used bread and wine to show them what would happen to His body. Today the church continues to share the Lord's Supper as a way of remembering Jesus' death.

FIND IT

Get permission from a parent to write in your Bible. Grab a highlighter and your Bible, and highlight any important words from these two stories: Jesus' baptism in Matthew 3:13-17 and the first Lord's Supper in 1 Corinthians 11:23-26.

FOLLOWING JESUS' EXAMPLE

LEARN IT

Start with this dove and draw a trail that tells what happened after Jesus was baptized.

PRAY IT

If you are nervous about being baptized, talk with a parent and pray together, asking God to give you courage.

Imagine you were John. How would you feel if Jesus came to you and asked you to baptize Him? John felt that he needed to be baptized by Jesus instead of being the one to baptize Jesus. Jesus said John needed to baptize Him to help Him fulfill what God had sent Him to do. Jesus set an example for Christians to follow through His baptism.

The first churches baptized because of the example Jesus gave them and also because He commanded them to do so. This week's memory verse helps you know what happens when you obey Jesus. Do you remember the memory verse? (If you don't, review your card from yesterday.) It says to obey what Jesus commanded.

What happened when Jesus came out of the water? (Read Matthew 3:16-17.)

❓ **How did God respond to Jesus?**

❓ **How did your family respond when you became a Christian?**

❓ **Who was the first person you told when you became a Christian?**

"AND THERE CAME A VOICE FROM HEAVEN: THIS IS MY BELOVED SON. I TAKE DELIGHT IN HIM!"

MATTHEW 3:17

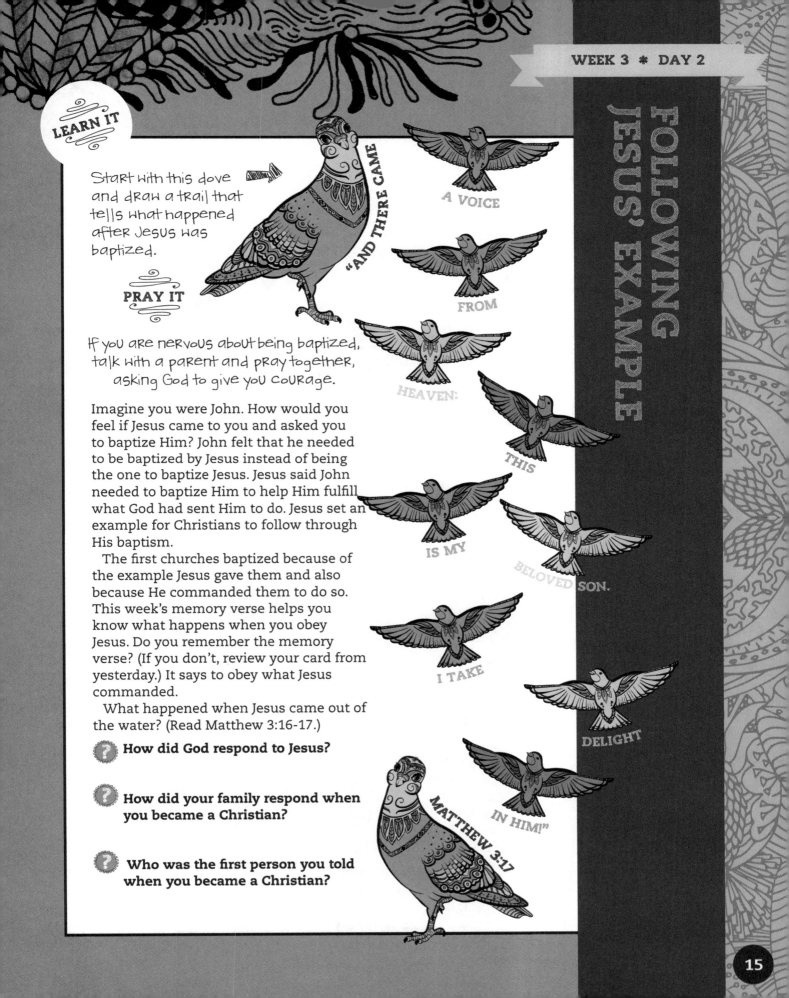

15

FOLLOWING JESUS' EXAMPLE

LEARN IT

Each of the following words is missing a vowel. Replace them to see all the different places where people can get baptized!

A E I O U

L_K_

SW_MM_NG P__L

CH_RCH B__PT_STRY

R_V_R

BONUS:
Did you know missionaries sometimes have to baptize people in a

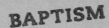

BAPTISM

Baptism shows that a person has turned away from the way he used to live, has asked Jesus into his life, and wants to follow Jesus every day. Becoming a Christian comes first—baptism does not make a person a Christian. The act of baptism is a reminder of Jesus' death, burial, and resurrection. When a person is baptized, he is immersed in water. (Immersed means to be put under water completely.)

LIVE IT

Ask a parent or senior adult to tell you about his baptism. Let him tell you where he was baptized and who baptized him. Write the answers here:

FOLLOWING JESUS' EXAMPLE

Many important words about the Lord's Supper are in 1 Corinthians 11:23–26. Read the verses with a parent and then search for the words below. Want an extra challenge? Find the words that are in the puzzle twice!

LEARN IT

1 JOHN 2:6

Do you remember our key verse from this week? Write down as much of it as you can without looking. Then, check your work by looking at 1 John 2:6.

FIND IT

BLOOD		OFTEN
BODY	CUP	PROCLAIM
BREAD	JESUS	REMEMBRANCE
BROKE	LORD	THANKS

```
B R O K E G N C A J Y K S P K
R H Y F A I Z E F Y X D J U J
E C N A R B M E M E R E O C B
T U I F F M S M K Y S W H B R
H R K X H R I E H U C L T D E
A N C U P O C A S Z X A O S A
N N W Q V T F B L V E O E K D
K V N S T P C T P C L K R N P
S N D I T Z Q M E B O R J A A
V H R Y S S G X C N F R D H H
D Z O B R O K E U O Q Z P T X
A V T Y L O R D J T O F T E N
E G D E K E J E S U S L K F E
R O R E M E M B R A N C E K R
B L O O D V U D R O L Y T C R
```

17

FOLLOWING JESUS' EXAMPLE

LEARN IT

During a baptism or the Lord's Supper, you should show respect for God and what He has done for you. Play the following game with a family member or a friend. Flip a coin onto the grid and tell if the picture shows something that is respectful (give a thumbs-up) or disrespectful (give a thumbs-down) to do during baptism or the Lord's Supper.

FIND IT

Grab your Bible and find 1 Corinthians 10:31. Tell a parent or friend how you plan to act during the next baptism or Lord's Supper at your church.

PRAY IT

Ask God to help you show respect and honor to Him during baptism and the Lord's Supper.

FIND IT

Read Acts 2:42 to find the four things the early church did together? Match those things with pictures you can do today. (Hint: "They devoted themselves to ...")

F_____

A_____ T_____

P_____

B_____ OF B_____

LIVE IT

The early church committed themselves TO LISTENING CLOSELY to the apostles' teaching. Where do you HEAR the teaching of the Bible in your church?

This week you will be learning about the church—what it is and what you can do as a part of the church. Aren't you glad there is a place you can go to meet with other people who believe in Jesus? Today churches gather to be able to learn more about God, Jesus, and the Bible. Every church is different. Even church buildings are different. Some churches meet in big buildings that have steeples and crosses. Other churches meet in school buildings. In Africa, some churches meet outside or under shelters that have grass roofs.

I'M PART OF A CHURCH

LEARN IT

Jesus gave specific instructions for His followers. Match each shape to a letter to find out what every baptized believer in the church should do.

EPHESIANS 6:20:

ACTS 22:15:

MATTHEW 28:19:

1 JOHN 4:7:

PHILIPPIANS 4:4:

What are three things you can do to help at your church right now? If you need ideas, talk to your parents or another adult from your church. They can help you think of ways to help. Write your answers below.

A	◉
B	☾
C	◎
D	♣
E	♥
F	★
G	✚
H	❀
I	🎆
J	🍃
K	◉
L	☺
M	◎
N	⚡
O	⠿
P	☆
Q	☀
R	→
S	←
T	☰
U	∿
V	◎
W	★
X	◉
Y	✹
Z	✿

LEARN IT

Answer each question or fill in the blank to find people who work together to help your church run smoothly.

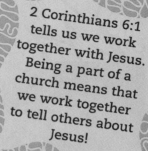
 WHO CLEANS YOUR CHURCH BUILDING?

 WRITE THE NAME OF A SUNDAY SCHOOL TEACHER (other than your own teacher).

 WHO PRINTS THE CHURCH BULLETINS?

 WHO PLAYS THE PIANO?

 WHO IS PREPARING TO GO ON A MISSION TRIP?

 WHO WELCOMES GUESTS AT THE FRONT DOOR?

 WRITE THE NAME OF A DEACON.

I'M PART OF A CHURCH

I'M PART OF A CHURCH

Interview someone in your family or neighborhood who is a member of your church.

LEARN IT

How long have you been a member of this church?

Name of person interviewed:

When did you trust Jesus to be your Savior?

How does our church help others?

Where were you baptized?

Have you ever served at church? What did you do?

What does being a church member mean to you?

PRAY IT   Thank God for your church family and pray specifically for the person you interviewed.

I'M PART OF A CHURCH

LIVE IT

Complete the map by drawing places you go in your community and writing their names in the space below. Using a different colored marker, write beside each location the name of a person you could tell about Jesus and how you can serve him.

DO IT

Ask a parent to help you make cookies and deliver them to a church member.

LIVING AS A CHRISTIAN

FIND IT

Find the following verses in the Bible and answer the questions.
John 14:15 • Exodus 20:3-17 • Matthew 22:36-39

What do you do if you love God?
_____

What are the 10 Commandments?
_____   _____
_____   _____
_____   _____
_____   _____
_____   _____

What are God's two most important commands?
_____   _____

LIVE IT

With an adult's help, think of someone who needs to know Jesus' love.

Write his/her name here: _____
What can you do to show love to that person? Circle an idea below and ask your parent to help you do it.

Bake Cookies

Rake leaves

Read a book to her

Help him wash his car

Walk her dog

Tell him about Jesus

LIVING AS A CHRISTIAN

What are some ways you can live like Jesus? Use the picture clues to help you.

LEARN IT

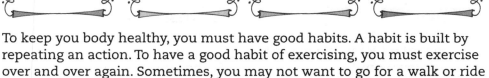

To keep you body healthy, you must have good habits. A habit is built by repeating an action. To have a good habit of exercising, you must exercise over and over again. Sometimes, you may not want to go for a walk or ride your bike. Some exercises are difficult to learn! But you show discipline when you stick with your activity. Guess what? The activity becomes easier each time! Like you discipline your body to do good things, your heart needs discipline to live like Jesus too. So regularly give, read the Bible, pray, and worship.

GOOD NEWS!

WHAT IS THE GREATEST NEWS YOU HAVE EVER HEARD? Did you keep the news to yourself or did you tell it to someone else? Becoming a Christian is the greatest change that will ever take place in your life, and you need to tell others about it. You also need to tell other people how they can become a Christian. This week you will learn about how you can study your Bible to learn more about Jesus. When you study and learn more about Jesus, you will be able to tell other people about Him.

LIVING AS A CHRISTIAN

DO IT

WORD BANK:

Pray   Give
Worship   Study
Serve   Go
              Tell

DOWN
1. How you show God how important He is and how much you love Him.
2. How you talk to God.
3. What to do to teach people about God.

ACROSS:
4. How you get to people in other places.
5. Showing God's love by doing things to help others.
6. Read the Bible to learn what God says.
7. You can _____ your time, tithe, or talents.

 PRAY IT Dear God, Thank You for giving me Your Word. Please help me to do what it says and live more like Jesus.

WHAT'S WORSHIP?

 LEARN IT
Worship means _____.
I can pray about _____.
I can give by _____.
Studying the Bible teaches _____.

LIVING AS A CHRISTIAN

Write the letter in the center of the letter box in the first blank. Then move in the direction of the arrow for the number of spaces listed beside it. Write each letter to find the secret message.

C I D B V
A L G S T
S Y I A N
H E B W O
W O Y E G

 DO IT
START

I   C A N
↑2←2 ↓1 →4↓1

[ ] [ ] [ ]   [ ] [ ] [ ]
↑1←1 ↓2←3 →4 ↓1←4   ↑3→2 ↓3←1 ↑4→1

[ ] [ ] [ ] [ ]   [ ] [ ]   [ ] [ ] [ ] [ ]
↓1←1 ↓3 ↑4→3 ↓4←1   ↑1←1 ↓1   ↑4 ↓3→2 ↑1←2 →2 ↑1←2

[ ] [ ] [ ] [ ]   [ ] [ ]   [ ] [ ] [ ] [ ] .
↓2→1 ←3 ↑1→3 ↑1→1   ↓2←4 ↓1→3   ↑2←3 ↑1 ↓3→2 ↑3→1

 **LIVE IT** TRUE OR FALSE? Circle T or F beside each statement. If false, write what God's word teaches on the line below it.

T F If I break mom's favorite lamp, I should blame it on the dog.

_____

T F Adam was really mean to me at recess. I should be nice to him anyway.

_____

T F I really like Marie's new red pen. I shouldn't take it, but I could ask nicely to use it.

_____

T F Dad said I can't ride my bike to the park. Dad isn't home now, so I can go to the park. I'll just come back before he gets home from work.

_____

T F Loving God is the most important thing. It is also important that I love others.

LIVING AS A CHRISTIAN

FIND IT

Read Philippians 4:13 and write it below.

According to the verse, can you do what God teaches in His Word?

If so, how can you do those things?

Although God already knows everything about you, you still have lots of things to learn about God. You get to know God when you spend time with Him. God wants you to talk with Him and tell Him what you're thinking, how you're feeling, what your dreams are, and what your needs are. Spending time with God means spending time reading your Bible and praying.

PRAY IT

Dear God, Thank You for teaching me to live as a Christian by giving me Your Word. Give me the strength to do Your commands.

SHARING YOUR TESTIMONY

Read Luke 19:1-10. When Zacchaeus met Jesus, he suddenly changed. He told the crowd that he wanted to do right things. He became the opposite of what he was. Unscramble the words on the right to discover how Jesus changed Zacchaeus's heart.

FIND IT

SELFISH ➡ RNEGUSOE ___ ___ ___ ___ ___ ___ ___ ___

HARDHEARTED ➡ RNICAG ___ ___ ___ ___ ___ ___

PROUD ➡ HLEFLUP ___ ___ ___ ___ ___ ___ ___

MEAN ➡ NKID ___ ___ ___ ___

LEARN IT

What is a testimony? Find the hidden words in the border on the edge of the page, and color them according to the code below. Then write the words you've colored in the box with the matching color.

- 2 letter word
- 3-letter word used to ask questions
- The Savior
- 4-letter word that begins with "y"
- 5-letter word that is a noun
- The opposite of death
- 7-letter word that ends with "g"
- Means "became different"
- the most common 3-letter word
- Rhymes with "jazz"

GIVING A TESTIMONY IS

PRAY IT Write your prayer of thanks to God here:

LEARN IT Several important steps happened before, during, and after the time you decided to ask Jesus to be your Savior. These rhymes will help you remember those steps. Write the word on the line, then try to find it in the puzzle.

➡ God is superior in the universe; rhymes with ring: _____

➡ God gave rules to protect people; rhymes with expands: _____

➡ I did wrong; rhymes with chin: _____

➡ I felt bad and embarrassed about my wrongdoing; rhymes with fame: _____

➡ To feel better, sometimes I would say untrue things; rhymes with pie: _____

➡ To feel better, sometimes I would try to do what I should; rhymes with hood: _____

➡ I realized I could not save myself; rhymes with bead: _____

➡ I heard the story that Jesus gave His life for me; rhymes with floss: _____

➡ I heard that Jesus could erase my sins; rhymes with outlive: _____

➡ I wanted to change; rhymes with air-vent: _____

➡ I told Jesus I knew He was the Son of God; rhymes with achieve: _____

➡ I told God I was sorry for my sins; rhymes with a mess: _____

➡ I did this to trust Jesus as Savior; rhymes with gray: _____

➡ I am learning to do His will each day; rhymes with hollow: _____

➡ My attitudes and actions are different; rhymes with range: _____

➡ I like to share my testimony; rhymes with glory: _____

```
Z I Y J I U A C I L I T G V F
L L J R L M J H V M D J S H B
S V O O O R R A A M E V S G X
D S E I L T Q N G N F S O O I
W D V C C B S G X O E X R O L
T N E P E R K E L F W E C D E
M A C W I I Q L N S C X D K F
I M C J N X O O P R A Y P K J
K M Y G H W C J F X K E D M Y
I O B E L I E V E O M K P B Y
E C V X X U M R Q A R U E P G
F G R J Y I A N H Q J G K Y Y
O R P O H H W S I R L S I K E
W R X S H K U X M S Z Z V V Q
Y X V H K D A P B A E G Z L E
```

DO IT Tell someone your story of how Jesus became your Savior and Lord. This is your God Story!

SHARING YOUR TESTIMONY

FIND IT Read John 4:1-30, 39-42. The woman who met Jesus at the well had a testimony. She ran and told everyone in town about this special man who helped her understand more about God. Because of her, many people in her town decided to believe Jesus was the Savior. Do you want to be excited telling about your faith in Jesus, like this woman? Ask God to help you!

Shade in the footprints marked with a Z to complete the words in the prayer below.

FIND IT Dear God, help me to never forget how much You have done for me. My life was full of sin before. But Jesus set me _____. Jesus _____ me when I confessed my sin to Him. Make me _____ to tell people that your love and forgiveness are _____. Give me _____. Amen.

DO IT Draw pictures that help you remember parts of your God Story. Practice writing your story below these pictures. Or make up your own set of pictures to tell your testimony. Pictures and props add interest and give you more confidence as a storyteller.

SHARING YOUR TESTIMONY

DO IT How did you get to Jesus? Some people hear about Jesus from their parents. Some people go to camp with a friend. Some even learn about Jesus from a missionary who has traveled from far away. Write the names of people who helped you learn about Jesus.

LEARN IT The words to a great memory verse are scrambled below. Put the words to the memory verse in order. The shapes of the puzzle pieces will give you a hint. Learn the verse and say it to a parent.

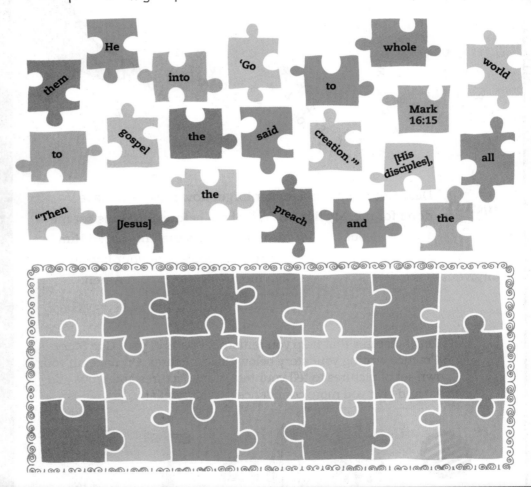

SHARING YOUR TESTIMONY

SHARING YOUR TESTIMONY

Match the sign beside the word to the sign under each line. Write the matching word in the blank.

 FIND IT Read Acts 4:1-20. After Jesus rose from the grave, He visited the disciples. He told the disciples to tell about God's love. Then He went to heaven to be with His Father. Right away, the disciples began to do the work Jesus asked them to do. They preached to big crowds in cities, and they answered people's questions about Jesus one-on-one. Some people listened and believed. Some people wanted them to stop. People told Peter and John not to talk about Jesus anymore. What was their answer? (Hint: see verse 20.)

 DO IT Circle the different places you can find opportunities to share your God Story. Put a star by the place you'd most like to go to share your testimony.

 CHURCH   NURSING HOME   PARK   HOSPITAL   FAIR   GAME

PRAY IT Find Acts 4:29. Do not be afraid of people who do not want you to talk about God. Remember that some people say they do not want to hear, but others will decide to believe if you explain all God has done for you. Do not give up. Keep sharing your testimony! Write the prayer that Peter and John prayed after the important people told them not to talk about Jesus:

GOING ON MISSION

Why be a Christian on Mission? Missionaries arrive at their destination many different ways. Missionaries travel by airplane, bus, canoe, and on foot. Choose the path that is the slowest, then cross out the first letter, and then every other letter in the path. Write each letter that remains in the blanks below to discover why Christians should want an on mission attitude.

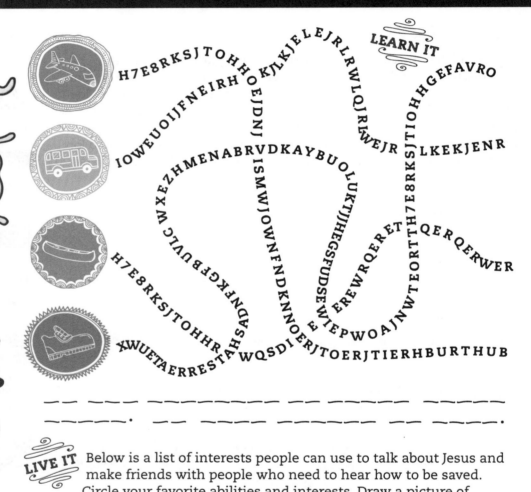

LEARN IT

H7E8RKSJTOHHOEJDNJ

IOWEUOIJFNEIRHHOKJLKJELEJRLRWLQJRWEJR LKEKJENR

WXEZHMENABRVDKAYBUOLUKTJJHEGSFUDSEWIEPWOAJNWTEORTH7E8RKSJTIOHHGEFAVRO

ISMWJOWNFNDKNNOERJTOERJTIERHBURTHUB QERQERWER

EREWRQERET

H7E8RKSJTOHHR WQSDI

XWUETAERRESTAHSADNPFKGFEBUVLC

_ _

_ _ _ _ _ . _

LIVE IT

Below is a list of interests people can use to talk about Jesus and make friends with people who need to hear how to be saved. Circle your favorite abilities and interests. Draw a picture of yourself making a new friend by doing your favorite thing. You can make a difference by telling others about Jesus!

ART	RUNNING	THEATER
FARMING	MEDICINE	BALL TEAMS
MUSIC	NURSING	CARS
COOKING	MOVIES	BIBLE STUDY
TEACHING	CRAFTS	WRITING
FISHING	SNOW SPORTS	PHOTOGRAPHY
COMPUTERS	TRAVELING	GARDENING

LEARN IT Look at the country flags. Under each flag, the country name is scrambled. See if you can unscramble the name and fill in the crossword puzzle.

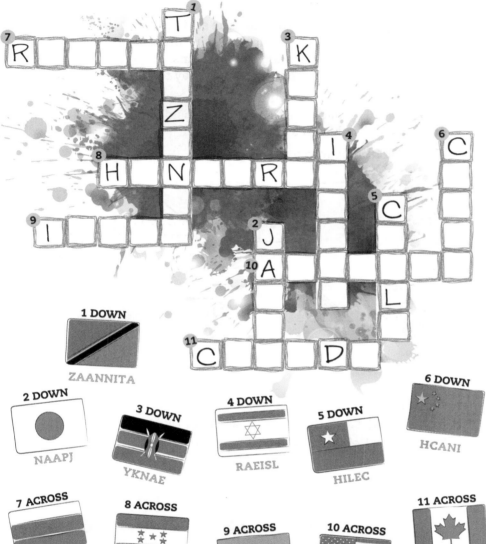

1 DOWN
ZAANNITA

2 DOWN
NAAPJ

3 DOWN
YKNAE

4 DOWN
RAEISL

5 DOWN
HILEC

6 DOWN
HCANI

7 ACROSS
IRSAUS

8 ACROSS
RASHUOND

9 ACROSS
DIAIN

10 ACROSS
CAAIMER

11 ACROSS
CAAAND

PRAY IT Ask God to send missionaries to these countries. Pray that many more people hear Jesus is the Way, the Truth, and the Life.

GOING ON MISSION

DO IT

FOLD A BOAT THAT TELLS ABOUT JESUS.

1. Use a permanent marker to write true sayings about Jesus all over a piece of paper. Here are some ideas: Jesus forgives sins. Jesus died on a cross to take the punishment for your sins. God loves people. He sent Jesus. Believing in Jesus is the only way to get into heaven.

2. Fold the paper into an origami boat, as shown below. Or roll up the paper you've decorated and push it inside a dry, empty water bottle. Make a sail from a straw and paper.

3. Send or sail the boat to a friend.

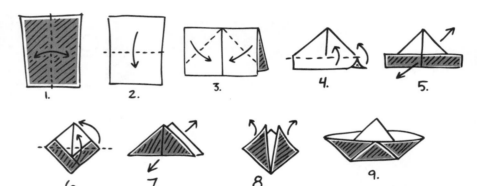

 FIND IT Find this week's Bible verse, Matthew 28:19a. Read it aloud. Look at the pictures and write the first letter of each word in a blank.

"G☐, T☐EREF☐RE, ☐ND M☐KE DISCI☐LES ☐F ☐LL N☐TI☐NS."

MATTHEW 28:19a

GOING ON MISSION

Some missionaries in South America hike high mountains to reach villages far away from cities. Why do they travel in harsh conditions to teach and preach about Jesus? Follow the steps below to finish the answer.

LEARN IT

The **first letter** is at the **peak** of the mountain.
The **second letter** is **southwest** of the first.
The **third letter** is **southeast** of the second.
The **fourth letter** is due **east** of the third.
The **fifth letter** is **southeast** of the fourth.
The **sixth letter** is due **west** of the fifth.

MISSIONARIES WANT PEOPLE TO HEAR ABOUT JESUS SO THEY HAVE THE

TO BELIEVE IN HIM, RECEIVE FORGIVENESS FOR SIN, AND GO TO HEAVEN FOR ETERNITY.

DO IT

Make a sticker or magnet that says Mission Monday. Every Monday this month, pray for missionaries or a specific country. Do extra chores to earn money for a mission offering. Think of something you can do for another person that might lead to the opportunity to talk about God's love. Some things might be raking leaves, fixing a care package for a local shelter, dropping off food at a food bank, or carrying your neighbor's mail to the door. You may be someone's chance to hear about Jesus.

MISSION MONDAY

GOING ON MISSION

FIND IT

Find Romans 10:14. Read the verse aloud. Find what the world needs most by drawing a line from the lands with the words to the lands inside the world. Write the words from the numbered lands in the numbered spaces below.

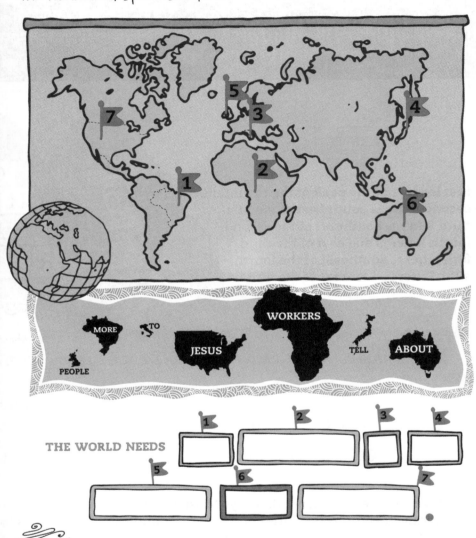

THE WORLD NEEDS

PRAY IT

Ask God for courage to tell others about Jesus. Ask God for wisdom to know what to say. Ask God to send more missionaries to all nations, so more people will hear the good news about Jesus.

TRAVELING ON

DO IT

Find the terms from the Word Bank in the word search below.

```
X F O R G I V E N E S S
A X B V Y L O Y D U T S F
S A C C E P T A N C E T B
K U L K G X U B C F S A L
G R O W L W N R N X S T X
U G V H A N B O P J R W O
D P E R F E C T I O Q Z A
L Y O T X V M F U L S F N
G P R A Y K Q W B N X E V
```

WORD BANK
love
forgiveness
confess
perfect
acceptance
purpose
study
grow
pray
ask

LEARN IT Fill in the blanks to complete the memory verse. Then write your memory verse on an index card and say it to an adult each day this week.

"THEREFORE, BE _____ OF _____, AS DEARLY LOVED _____."
—EPHESIANS 5:1

PRAY IT Dear God, help me to always turn to You when I have questions. Thank You for always being with me!

TRAVELING ON

FIND IT

Find and read the following verses to help you answer the questions and fill in the missing words. Think about the definitions of grace and mercy.

1. What is grace? **GETTING GOOD THINGS YOU DON'T DESERVE**

4. Acts 20:32 says that the message of grace can

2. Psalm 84:11 says that the Lord grace.

3. John 1:17 says that God gives grace through

5. What is mercy? **NOT GETTING PUNISHMENT YOU DESERVE**

6. Isaiah 30:18 says that the Lord will mercy.

8. Luke 1:50 says God's mercy lasts …

7. Matthew 5:7 says that God the merciful.

PRAY IT

Dear God, Help me to learn about the grace and mercy you've given me. Please help me to show grace and mercy to others.

God does not expect me to be _____; I will still mess up. But God _____ me when I _____ my sins to Him.

God's _____ and _____ can't be earned.

Jesus taught that the _____ of life is to love _____ and _____.

I am not perfect, but if I follow _____ example, I can live life God's way.

I can _____ by _____ the Bible, _____, and _____ questions from adults who know God.

No matter what, I should remember that God will always love me and is always _____ me.

WORD BANK
love
forgives
confess
perfect
acceptance
purpose
God
others
Jesus'
grow
studying
praying
asking
with

DO IT Answer the clues below, filling in the first letter on the inside of the shape. Then fill in each letter in the corresponding shape below to find a message about God.

Another word meaning "forever": [E] T E R N I T Y

Has 8 tentacles and lives in the sea: ◯ _ _ _ _ _ _ _

A person playing a character on stage or in a movie: ⬡ _ _ _ _ _

Frozen water is called: △ _ _ _

GOD △s ◯lw◯ys th[E]r[E] ◯nd H◻ will ◯lw◯ys lov◻ m◻.

TRAVELING ON

TRAVELING ON

LIVE IT

Think about questions you may have about life as a Christian. Make a list. Then sit down with an adult and ask him to help you answer the questions. Before you start, pray together that God would help you to understand.

FIND IT

Find Jeremiah 29:11–13. Fill in the blanks to learn more about God's plans. Use these words: hope, heart, plans, future, listen, all, you, Me, knows.

1. God has _____ for you. He already _____ them.

2. God wants to give you a _____ and a _____.

3. When you pray to God, He promises to _____ to you. How do you feel knowing God hears you? _____ _____

4. When you seek God, He says, "_____ will find _____."

5. You should search for God with _____ of your _____.

TRAVELING ON

Choose from the following words to help you find your answer: serve, tell, love, help.

LIVE IT

What is the goal of life as a Christian?

TO _____ AND _____ HIM, _____ OTHERS, AND _____ THEM TO DO THE SAME.

Because you are a Christian doesn't mean you will never sin again. It means you are forgiven for your sins as soon as you ask God for forgiveness. God still loves you, even when you mess up. He is never far away. He gives you strength to live for Him. How do you receive forgiveness from God?

_____

All people can receive forgiveness from God if they ask. When you pray and ask God to forgive you, don't forget your friends who need to know Him—pray for them, too!

Who do you know who needs to know Jesus? Write their names in the boxes below.

HOW Do I Study MY BIBLE?

STUDY ONE BIBLE BOOK.

WHO
wrote the book and
when was the book written?

WHAT
is the book about?

WHAT
does the book say about God?

WHAT
people does the book tell about?

HOW
did the people act toward God?

WHAT
can you learn about God
from the book?

STUDY ONE BIBLE VERSE.

READ
the verse from
different Bible translations.

WHAT
are the important words in the verse?

WHAT
are the words you don't understand?

WRITE
the verse in your own words.
What can you learn from the
verse?

STUDY ONE PERSON.

WHEN
and where did the
person live?

WHAT
took place in the person's life?

HOW
did the person act?

WHAT
can you learn from the person?

MAKING A
MY GOD STORY
BOX

You have a great memory, but sometimes having an object you can see will help you remember events better. If you don't create a box in class, you may want to make one at home. You can place items in the box that can help you remember the most important time in your life. As you look through this book, place items in your box that will help you remember what you learn.

CREATING THE BOX

PROVIDE:
- A plastic shoebox or an older child's or adult size shoe box.
- Craft paper to cover the box if needed
- Clear tape
- Markers, crayons, stickers, or other items to use to decorate the box

BOX

PAPER

TAPE

MARKERS

CRAYONS

STICKERS

TO DO:
- Use the supplies collected to decorate your box.
- Keep your box in a safe place and add items to it to help you remember when you trusted Jesus as your Savior and Lord and when you were baptized.
- Include your name on the box.

GOD RULES.

God came first. He always was. He is the King of the universe.

WE SINNED.

God created people to share His glory, life, and love. But we have all rebelled against Him. We want our own way. We do wrong things.

GOD PROVIDED.

God knew we would have a need to be rescued from our sin, He had a plan from before the beginning of time. He would send His only Son, Jesus, to become the sacrifice that would make people right with Him again.

JESUS GIVES.

At just the right time, God sent Jesus. Jesus did what no human could do. He lived a perfect life. He said yes to everything God asked Him to do. He never did anything wrong. People were not nice to Him. When He died on a cross, He was taking the punishment for the sins of all people. Because Jesus died on the cross and rose again, He alone has permission to erase sin from the hearts of people who believe in Him and trust Him to forgive them.

WE RESPOND.

Each person who hears the truth about Jesus gets to decide to respond by welcoming Him into her life or by ignoring what she has learned. It is sad when people walk away from God's offer to save them, but people do it every day. You can't force people to believe. You can pray for your friends and family who don't believe and tell them how Jesus has changed you. People must realize they need Jesus before they can respond to Him.